History Highlights

TIMELINE *of the* CLASSICAL WORLD

By Charlie Samuels

Gareth Stevens
Publishing

Please visit our Web site www.garethstevens.com. For a free color catalog of all our high-quality books, call toll free 1-800-542-2595 or fax 1-877-542-2596.

Library of Congress Cataloging-in-Publication Data
Samuels, Charlie, 1961-
    Timeline of the classical world / Charlie Samuels.
        p. cm. — (History highlights)
    Includes index.
    ISBN 978-1-4339-3480-3 (library binding) — ISBN 978-1-4339-3481-0 (pbk.)
    ISBN 978-1-4339-3482-7 (6-pack)
    1. Civilization, Classical—Juvenile literature. I. Title.
    CB311.S25 2010
    938—dc22   2009037151

Published in 2010 by
Gareth Stevens Publishing
111 East 14th Street, Suite 349
New York, NY 10003

© 2010 The Brown Reference Group Ltd.

For Gareth Stevens Publishing:
Art Direction: Haley Harasymiw
Editorial Direction: Kerri O'Donnell

For The Brown Reference Group Ltd:
Editorial Director: Lindsey Lowe
Managing Editor: Tim Cooke
Editor: Ben Hollingum
Children's Publisher: Anne O'Daly
Design Manager: David Poole
Designer: Karen Perry
Picture Manager: Sophie Mortimer
Production Director: Alastair Gourlay

Picture Credits:
Front Cover: istockphoto

Jupiter Images: Ablestock: 34; Photos.com: 5, 6, 7b, 10, 11, 15, 19, 20, 21r, 23t, 25t, 28, 29, 35t, 40, 45; Stockxpert: 8, 9b, 13, 14, 22, 31b, 33t, 36, 38, 42, 43t; Shutterstock: Oleg Babich: 26; PPL: 18; Vladimir Wrangel 25b

All Artworks Brown Reference Group

Publisher's note to educators and parents: Our editors have carefully reviewed the Web sites that appear on p. 47 to ensure that they are suitable for students. Many Web sites change frequently, however, and we cannot guarantee that a site's future contents will continue to meet our high standards of quality and educational value. Be advised that students should be closely supervised whenever they access the Internet.

Manufactured in the United States of America
1 2 3 4 5 6 7 8 9 12 11 10

CPSIA compliance information: Batch #BRW0102GS: For further information contact Gareth Stevens, New York, New York at 1-800-542-2595.

Contents

Introduction

Few periods of history have had a longer-lasting influence than the so-called classical age, when culture flourished in ancient Greece and ancient Rome.

The ancient civilizations of Greece and Rome had a huge influence on Western history. Athens in Greece was renowned as the home of democracy. Philosophers such as Socrates, Aristotle, and Plato were studied throughout the Middle Ages. Greek statues and architecture inspired the Renaissance in Italy. The ideals of the Roman republic underlay the American and French revolutions of the late 18th century.

Greece and Rome

Greek history began centuries before classical times, when the Mycenaeans dominated the eastern Mediterranean. When the Greek city-states emerged, they celebrated the past as an age of heroes. In classical Greece, conflict between Athens, Sparta, and other territories was broken only by periods of alliance against Persia until the young Macedonian king Alexander emerged to build an empire across most of Central Asia. Alexander's empire died with him. Meanwhile, in central Italy the citizens of Rome began a period of expansion based on military strength. From the Italian peninsula, their territory eventually spread around the Mediterranean Sea and throughout Europe. After centuries of dominance, the empire was split apart by internal divisions.

About This Book

This book focuses on the Classical World from the Dark Ages of Greek history in about 750 B.C.E. until shortly after the fall of Rome in 476 C.E. It contains two different types of timelines. Along the bottom of the pages is a timeline that covers the whole period. It lists key events and developments, color-coded by region. Each chapter also has its own timeline, running vertically down the sides of the pages. This timeline provides more specific details about the particular subject of the chapter.

Classical civilizations
built many
monumental
structures, many
of which still
stand today. ⤓

Homer's Greece

Around 2000 B.C., Greek culture was not very advanced.
But the period is still famous today because of the epic
poems of the poet Homer, who lived about 800 years later.

This vase shows two heroes of the war between the Greeks and the Trojans. →

TIMELINE
750–690 B.C.

750 B.C. The Archaic period of Greek history begins.

738 Midas becomes king of Phrygia in central Anatolia.

734 Greeks from Corinth set up a new colony at Syracuse, in Siciliy.

750   740   730

KEY:

EUROPE

ASIA

AFRICA

750 The ruler of Nubia takes over Lower Egypt.

744 Tiglath Pileser III becomes king of Assyria. He builds it into a mighty empire.

732 Damascus becomes part of the Assyrian empire.

727 Sargon II becomes king of Assyria. His power spreads over much of the Middle East.

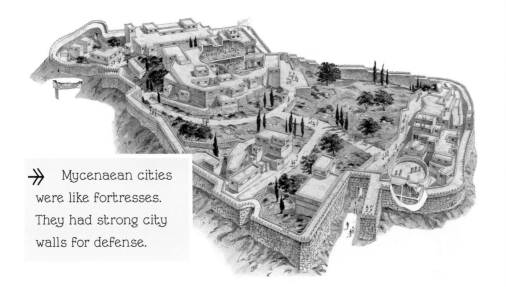

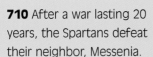 Mycenaean cities were like fortresses. They had strong city walls for defense.

The first significant civilization of mainland Greece emerged in about 1600 B.C. Its capital was at Mycenae on the Pelopennese, a peninsula that forms the southern part of the Greek mainland. The ruins excavated there suggest that the people were warlike, yet the Mycenaeans were also traders. Soldiers and traders worked together to spread Mycenae's influence across the eastern Mediterranean region.

The Collapse of Mycenae

The civilization's glory did not last for long; by 1250 B.C. it had collapsed. Historians still do not understand the reasons for its fall. A time of troubles was affecting the eastern Mediterranean. Egyptian records of the time refer to the "Sea Peoples," a mysterious group of peoples who were

c.2300 B.C. Immigrants from Anatolia bring Bronze Age culture to Greece.

c.2000 The first Minoan palaces are built in Crete.

c.1600 The Mycenaean civilization emerges in mainland Greece.

c.1450 Mount Thera erupts. It destroys some cities of Minoan Crete.

c.1250 The Mycenaean civilization collapses.

1184 Traditional date of the Fall of Troy.

c.1050 Dorians invade Greece from the north and bring ironworking.

← Homer's epics described the legendary Trojan Wars.

710 After a war lasting 20 years, the Spartans defeat their neighbor, Messenia.

707 Sargon II conquers Babylon.

700 The Etruscans begin to use written inscriptions.

710

700

690

700 The poet Hesiod writes *Theogony*, about the origins of the Greek gods.

690 The Assyrian king Sennacherib rebuilds the ancient city of Nineveh.

Timeline (continued)

c.1000 Greek settlers start to establish colonies on the Aegean's eastern coast.

776 The first Olympic Games are held at Olympia.

c.750 Greece's Archaic period begins; the first city-states date from this time.

c.750 The first evidence of a Greek alphabet comes from this period.

c.750 The great epics of Homer are composed (but they are not yet written down).

c.734 The first Greek colonies are founded in Sicily.

c.700 The poet Hesiod's *Theogony* records traditional stories of the Greek gods.

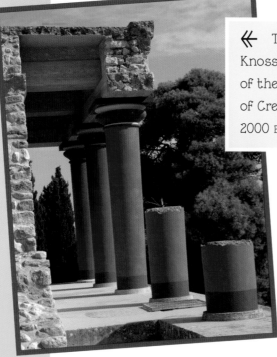

← The palace at Knossos was the heart of the Minoan culture of Crete from about 2000 B.C. to 1400 B.C.

looking for a new home. Even if the Sea Peoples did not destroy Mycenae itself, their activities would certainly have disrupted its trading network in the Mediterranean.

No new civilization arose to take Mycenae's place. Instead, local warlords fought over a land of scattered settlements. Later scholars described the years from 1250 B.C. to 850 B.C. as Greece's "Dark Age." In fact, we have no way of knowing how bleak it really was for those who lived through it.

Recovery

By the eighth century B.C., the outlook was much brighter. The growing wealth of successful local rulers encouraged craft industries and trade. That created perfect conditions for the evolution of the *polis*. This was a self-governing city-state, often consisting of little more than one large community and the countryside around it. Young adventurers from these cities founded trading

TIMELINE
690–630 B.C.

683 Hereditary kings in Athens are replaced by elected officials.

673 Astrologers in Babylon correctly predict an eclipse of the Sun.

690   680   670

KEY:

EUROPE

ASIA

AFRICA

689 The Assyrians sack Babylon after a Babylonian revolt.

665 The Kushites are driven out of Egypt, but still rule most of Nubia.

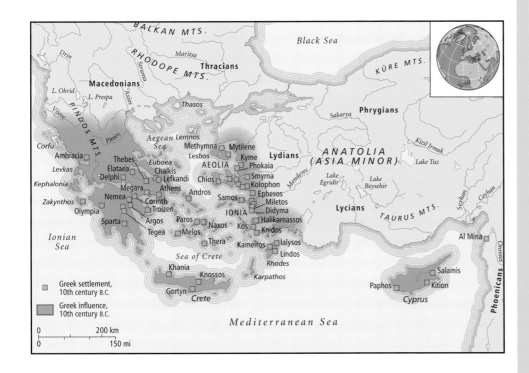

Greek settlement,
10th century B.C.

Greek influence,
10th century B.C.

The Minoans

The Minoan culture flourished from around 2000 B.C. on the island of Crete. The culture took its name from King Minos, whose name also lived on in myths of the Minotaur, a bull-headed monster that lived in a maze. The Minoans grew rich through trade but were devastated by a volcanic eruption in about 1450 B.C. Crete was conquered by Mycenaean Greeks by about 1400 B.C.

⇑ From the eleventh century B.C., Greeks settled on Aegean islands and the shores of Asia Minor.

posts abroad, enriching their home states even further. Among the cities, a sense of a common Greek identity was growing, too. It was encouraged by shared stories of gods and heroes. Almost nothing is known about Homer (he may even have been more than one poet), but his epics, the *Iliad* and the *Odyssey*, inspired the Greeks of future generations. They looked back to the period as a golden age.

This water carrier was painted on the walls of the palace at Knossos. ⇒

c.650 Many Greek city-states are taken over by rulers known as "tyrants."

650 Traditional date of the founding of the kingdom of Macedon.

650

640

630

654 The Phoenicians found colonies on the Balearic Islands in the western Mediterranean.

c.640 Persia becomes a state of the kingdom of the Medes.

The Etruscans in Italy

The Etruscans of central Italy are a mysterious people. What we know of their history has come down to us through the unflattering comments of Greek and Roman writers.

The Etruscans built their towns on the hilltops of the Tuscany region. ⟫

TIMELINE
630–570 B.C.

621 The politician Draco draws up a strict code of laws for Athens. "Draconian" still means harshly strict.

616 Etruscan kings begin to rule Rome.

604 Nebuchadrezzar II becomes king of Babylon and turns it again into a powerful empire.

630

620

610

KEY:

EUROPE

ASIA

AFRICA

626 B.C. Nabopolassar, governor of Babylon, rebels against the Assyrians and starts the Chaldean dynasty.

612 The Assyrian Empire is overthrown by a combination of Medes and Babylonians.

600 Coins are introduced in the Greek mainland.

Etruria was an area that roughly matched the modern Italian region of Tuscany. It was rich in iron and copper ores, and its coastline had many natural harbors. The Etruscans were skilled metalworkers and sailors. They grew rich by trading iron ingots, bronze, and other goods in their ships up and down the coast of Italy and across to southern France. By about 800 B.C., when Rome was still a hilltop cluster of huts, the Etruscans had already begun to live in cities.

Competition for Trade

Etruscan traders in the western Mediterranean faced competition. Phoenicians and Greeks also traded in the region. In about 600 B.C., the Greeks founded a trading colony at Massilia (modern Marseille) in southern France. From this base, they were able to seize control of the Rhone River. The river was a valuable trade route for boats into the heart of Europe. In response to the Greeks' growing power, the Etruscans formed an alliance with the trading city of Carthage in North Africa.

Timeline of Etruscan History

c.900 B.C. The Villanova culture of northern Italy uses iron.

c.800 Etruscan ships begin to voyage along the coast of Italy.

c.700 The first use of Etruscan alphabetic script.

c.616 An Etruscan, Tarquin I, becomes king of Rome.

c.600 Twelve Etruscan cities come together to form the Etruscan League.

c.550 The Etruscans gain control of the Po Valley north of Etruria.

539 Etruscans and their allies defeat the Greeks and halt the western spread of Greek colonies. The Etruscans take control of Corsica.

⬅ A sculpture in an Etruscan tomb shows the dead couple embracing on a couch.

586 Nebuchadrezzar II conquers Jerusalem and takes many captives to Babylon.

585 The Greek astronomer Thales predicts an eclipse of the Sun.

573 Nebuchadrezzar II conquers the Phoenician port of Tyre.

590

580

570

594 Solon becomes tyrant of Athens and begins to introduce a form of democracy.

578 Tarquin I, the first Etruscan king of Rome, dies.

Timeline (continued)

c.525 The Etruscans establish settlements in southern Italy.

510 Romans expel Tarquin II, the last Etruscan king of Rome.

504 The Etruscans suffer a major defeat at Aricia in southern Italy.

c.400 Gauls (Celts) cross the Alps to settle in the Po Valley. Etruscan power in the region begins to decline.

396 The Romans capture the city of Veii in southern Etruria after a 10-year war.

296–295 After a series of defeats, most Etruscan cities sign a truce with Rome.

285–280 Rome puts down a series of rebellions in the Etruscan cities.

An Advanced People

The Etruscans were technologically advanced and built roads, bridges, and canals. They adopted the alphabet, vase painting, and temple building from the Greeks. In

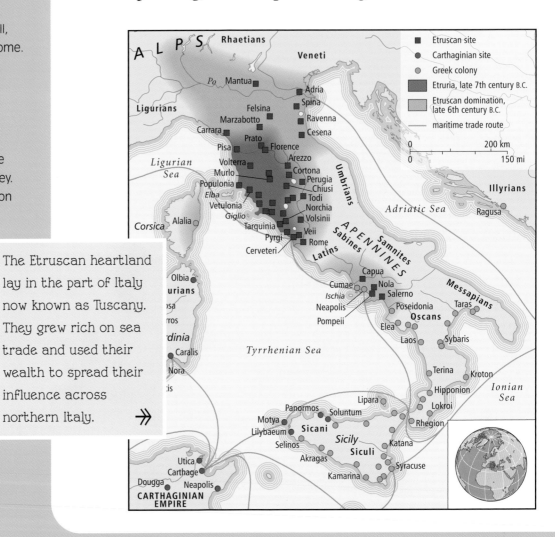

The Etruscan heartland lay in the part of Italy now known as Tuscany. They grew rich on sea trade and used their wealth to spread their influence across northern Italy. →

TIMELINE
570–510 B.C.

561 Peisistratus becomes tyrant of Athens. He dominates the city-state for 34 years.

558 Cyrus becomes king of Persia.

550 Cyrus defeats the Medes, beginning the rise of the Persian Empire.

570

560

550

562 Nebuchadrezzar II dies, ending the great days of the Neo-Babylonian Empire.

560 Croesus becomes king of Lydia in Anatolia (modern Turkey); he is famous for his wealth.

547 Cyrus defeats Croesus and brings all of Asia Minor under Persian rule.

KEY:

EUROPE

ASIA

AFRICA

the sixth century B.C., the Etruscans expanded north and south from Etruria. They even ruled Rome for a time. The major Etruscan cities formed a loose political alliance, or "league" of states.

← Etruscan tombs were like houses built of stone or carved out of rock.

Rome Takes Over

A group of Roman aristocrats overthrew the last Etruscan king of Rome in 510 B.C. The event was seen as the beginning of the Roman Republic. The Romans now gradually replaced the Etruscans as the dominant power in Italy. Early in the third century B.C., the Etruscans disappeared from history.

The Romans took many ideas from the Etruscans. They included augury—telling the future by observing natural phenomena such as the flight of birds. They also inherited the Etruscans' knowledge of engineering and metalwork, and even some military tactics.

← The Etruscans were skilled potters. They passed their skills on to the Romans.

Cities of the Dead

The Etruscans buried their dead in large cemeteries laid out almost like cities. Tombs often contained a sculpted model of a dead husband and wife lying together on a couch. The tombs held huge numbers of Greek vases, together with chariots and goods of gold, ivory, and amber. The goods show the wealth of the Etruscan nobles buried in the tombs.

530 Cyrus dies; he is replaced by his son Cambyses.

525 Cambyses conquers Egypt.

510 Tarquin II is expelled from Rome, ending the line of Etruscan kings.

530 520 510

540 The Peloponnesian League unites most Greek cities in an alliance led by Sparta.

521 Cambyses dies; Darius becomes ruler of Persia.

510 Cleisthenes replaces the tyranny in Athens with democracy.

The Greek City-States

At the start of the fifth century B.C., the Greek world was divided among city-states—cities that controlled nearby territory and had their own government.

The Parthenon stands on the high Acropolis that dominates the city of Athens. →

TIMELINE
510–450 B.C.

508 Etruscans make a last attempt to restore their rule in Rome.

494 The Romans form an assembly to represent their interests in the city's government.

490 The Greeks defeat the Persians at the Battle of Marathon.

510

500

490

KEY:

EUROPE

ASIA

AFRICA

509 B.C. Traditional date of the founding of the Roman Republic.

499 The Greek cities of Ionia rebel against Persian rule.

480 A new Persian leader, Xerxes, tries but fails to conquer Greece.

By 500 B.C. the two leading city-states in Greece were Sparta and Athens. Sparta was a militaristic state. At age seven, all boys were taken away from their families and brought up to be the soldiers of the future. Sparta had used its great military strength to acquire political control over a large part of the Peloponnese, a large peninsula in southern Greece.

⤒ The greatest sculptors in Greece helped build the Acropolis in Athens.

The Story of Athens

Athens stood on the coast near the neck of land leading to the Peloponnese. It had grown rich on seaborne trade. It was a democracy. Athenian citizens voted about important issues such as whether to declare war. However, Athenian democracy had some limitations: Citizenship was restricted to free men aged at least 20 who were born in Athens and whose parents were Athenians. Women, slaves, and foreigners could not become citizens.

Timeline of Greek City-States

490 B.C. King Darius of Persia invades Greece, but is defeated by the Athenians at Marathon.

480 Spartans fail to halt a new Persian invasion. The Persians take Athens, but are defeated in the Battle of Salamis.

479 A Spartan and Athenian army defeats the Persians at Plataea.

478 Athens leads a league of Greek cities against Persia; Sparta withdraws from the alliance against Persia.

⤓ Greek and Persian warriors fought in a number of battles.

474 The Etruscans suffer defeat in a naval battle at Cumae in southern Italy.

457 War breaks out between Athens and Sparta.

470   460   450

460 Birth of Hippocrates, a Greek physician who is known as the "father of medicine."

451 New laws extend legal protection to all Roman citizens.

Timeline (continued)

461 Pericles comes to power in Athens and begins a series of reforms.

457–445 The First Peloponnesian War breaks out between Athens and Sparta.

448 The Parthenon is built to celebrate the Athenian victory over the Persians.

431 Hostilities are renewed between Athens and Sparta (the Second Peloponnesian War).

430 Socrates begins teaching in Athens.

416 The Athenians lead an expedition against the island of Sicily, but withdraw in 413.

405 The Spartans defeat the Athenian fleet, spelling the end of Athens as a major power.

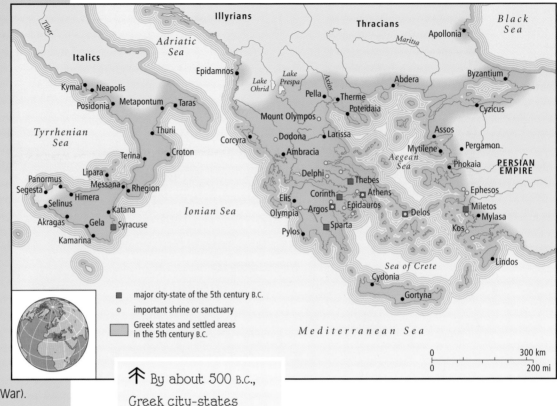

⬆ By about 500 B.C., Greek city-states controlled land from Asia Minor to Italy.

Some centuries earlier, colonists from Greece had founded a number of city-states along the Aegean coast of Asia Minor (present-day Turkey). The Greeks called the region Ionia. The Ionian cities had been ruled by Persia since the mid-sixth century B.C. When they rebelled against the Persian Empire in 499 B.C., Athens and other mainland city-states came to their aid.

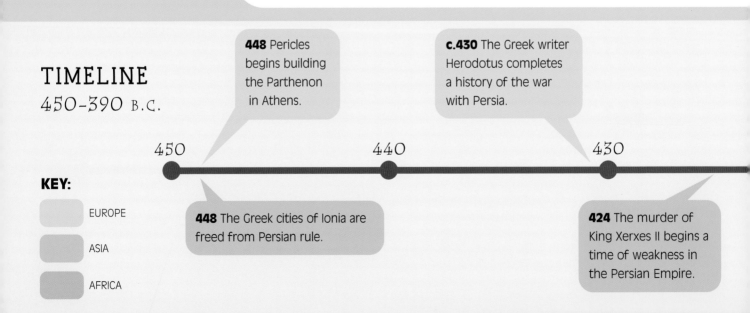

TIMELINE
450–390 B.C.

448 Pericles begins building the Parthenon in Athens.

c.430 The Greek writer Herodotus completes a history of the war with Persia.

450   440   430

KEY:

EUROPE

ASIA

AFRICA

448 The Greek cities of Ionia are freed from Persian rule.

424 The murder of King Xerxes II begins a time of weakness in the Persian Empire.

A Time of Warfare

The Persian King Darius used force to stop the uprising in the Ionian cities. He then gathered a huge army and navy to punish the rebels' supporters across the Aegean Sea in Greece. In all, the Persians sent three invasion forces to Greece between 492 B.C. and 480 B.C. Each time, the Persians were driven back by the courage of the much smaller Greek armies pitted against them.

The fear of invasion united Sparta and Athens; but once the Persian threat disappeared, the old rivalry between the two returned stronger than ever. Both Sparta and Athens wanted to dominate Greece. For 75 years, their quarrels plunged them and the rest of Greece into a series of conflicts, known as the Peloponnesian Wars. Although Greek culture continued to flourish, the constant wars weakened Greece politically and economically.

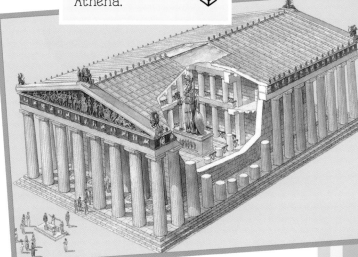

The Parthenon housed a huge golden statue of the goddess Athena. ⇓

The Classical Age

Scholars call the fifth century B.C. Greece's "Classical Age." Architecture, literature, art, and science flourished.

Artists and sculptors adorned the city with magnificent monuments, including the Parthenon. Citizens went to the theater to see plays by writers such as Aeschylus and Sophocles.

The plays are still performed today. Thinkers like Socrates and (in the fourth century B.C.) Plato and Aristotle raised philosophy to a new height.

---

404 The Egyptians rebel against Persian rule and become more or less independent.

399 Socrates is accused of corrupting young people in Athens with his teaching; he is forced to drink poison.

410   400   390

c.420 The Nabateans begin a kingdom in western Arabia with its capital at Petra, in what is now Jordan.

401 A Greek army is stranded in the middle of Persia, but fights its way back to Greece.

396 Rome captures the Etruscan city of Veii.

Aristotle

Few figures in history have influenced so many different areas of learning as Aristotle. His influence dominated European thought into the Middle Ages and beyond.

Aristotle's ideas formed the basis of modern Western philosophy. →

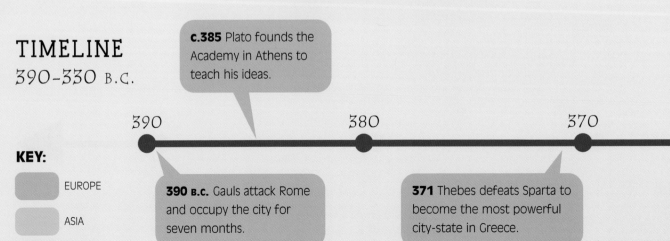

TIMELINE
390–330 B.C.

c.385 Plato founds the Academy in Athens to teach his ideas.

390   380   370

KEY:

- EUROPE
- ASIA
- AFRICA

390 B.C. Gauls attack Rome and occupy the city for seven months.

371 Thebes defeats Sparta to become the most powerful city-state in Greece.

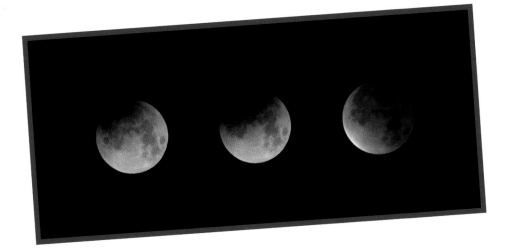

← The curved shadow cast by Earth on the Moon during an eclipse showed Aristotle that the Earth must be round.

Timeline of Aristotle's Life

384 B.C. Aristotle is born at Stagirus in Macedonia.

367 Studies at Plato's Academy in Athens.

347 Leaves Athens to travel and study.

342 Becomes tutor to Alexander of Macedon.

336 Alexander becomes king of Macedon; Aristotle returns to Athens.

335 Aristotle founds the Lyceum.

323 Alexander dies; Aristotle retreats to Chalcis.

322 Aristotle dies in Chalcis.

Aristotle was one of the most influential thinkers ever to have lived. He was born in 384 B.C. in Macedonia. Both his parents died while Aristotle was young. In 367 B.C., the boy's guardian sent him to Athens to study at the Academy of the philosopher Plato.

Studying and Teaching

After Plato died in 348 B.C., Aristotle traveled in Asia Minor and studied natural history. He then spent six years tutoring Alexander of Macedon, the future Alexander the Great. Aristotle returned to Athens and set up a school of his own, the Lyceum. It was also called the Peripatetic School, because Aristotle lectured while walking in the garden (*peripatetic* means "wandering"). In 323 B.C., Aristotle moved to Chalcis (modern Khalkis) on the island of Euboea, his mother's birthplace. He died there in 322 B.C.

348 Rome makes a treaty with Carthage not to attack one another.

343 Rome goes to war against its neighbors, the Samnites; within 50 years, it is the major power in central Italy.

336 Philip II is murdered; he is replaced by his son Alexander.

350

340

330

c.350 Greek sculptors build a tomb for King Mausolus at Halicarnassus; the Mausoleum becomes one of the wonders of the ancient world.

338 Philip II of Macedon defeats the Greeks and takes control of the city-states.

Plato's Academy

Aristotle's tutor Plato (c.428 B.C.–c.348 B.C.) was almost as influential as Aristotle. Plato himself had studied with another great philosopher, Socrates. Plato had many ideas about the nature of reality. The Academy he founded in Athens to spread his ideas among his students was the first center of higher education in the world.

The School of Athens was painted in A.D. 1510 by the Italian artist Raphael. It shows Plato, Aristotle, and others studying philosophical questions. →→

A Range of Interests

Aristotle's interests were wide. They included biology, physics, logic, philosophy, politics, meteorology, and cosmology. His rules remained the basis of the study of logic until the 19th century. In *Meteorologica*, he tried to explain weather phenomena; the work gave us our word "meteorology." One of Aristotle's failures was his understanding of the universe. He believed it consisted of a series of concentric spheres with Earth at the

TIMELINE
330-270 B.C.

323 The death of Alexander the Great begins a long power struggle for his empire.

305 Seleucus, one of Alexander's generals, begins the Seleucid kingdom in Persia and Mesopotamia.

330   320   310

KEY:

EUROPE

ASIA

AFRICA

c.330 The Greek Pytheas sails into the Atlantic and north as far as "Thule," which is probably what is now northern Norway.

305 Ptolemy, governor of Egypt, proclaims himself pharaoh.

center. He also accepted the theory that all matter is made up of four elements: earth, air, water, and fire. Aristotle added a fifth element, "aether," from which the heavens are made.

Aristotle proved that the Earth is round. He saw that, during a lunar eclipse, Earth casts a curved shadow on the Moon. He also noticed that, while traveling even a short distance north or south, new stars appear on one horizon while others disappear below the opposite horizon. Aristotle estimated the diameter of Earth and came within 50 percent of the correct value.

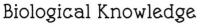

↓ Aristotle realized that dolphins were more like land animals than fish.

Biological Knowledge

Aristotle was most successful as a biologist. He classified more than 500 animal species and arranged them into groups. Noting that dolphins give birth to live babies, he classed them with land animals. Today, dolphins are recognized as mammals rather than fish.

Aristotle divided animals into those with blood and those without; today scientists make a similar split between vertebrates and invertebrates. He also compiled a "ladder of nature" that remained the basis of animal classification until the eighteenth century—it took no account of evolution, however.

↑ This image of Aristotle is from the Renaissance, when he was still an important philsopher.

c.300 The Greek mathematician Euclid outlines the principles of geometry.

287 Ordinary Romans are given equal rights with nobles.

279 Celts invade northern Greece and Macedonia.

290

280

270

c.300 Ptolemy founds a museum at Alexandria.

278 Celtic mercenaries form their own state, Galatia, in Asia Minor.

Alexander the Great

Greek power was carried deep into Asia by Alexander the Great, a military genius who defeated the Persian Empire and ranks among the greatest generals of all time.

← There are monuments to Alexander throughout his former empire.

TIMELINE
270–210 B.C.

c.250 Knowledge of ironworking spreads across the Sahara to sub-Saharan Africa.

241 After Roman victory in the First Punic War, Carthage loses its trading colonies in Siciliy.

270   260   250

KEY:

EUROPE

ASIA

AFRICA

264 B.C. Conflict breaks out between Rome and the North African city of Carthage, beginning the First Punic War.

247 The Parthians, warlike nomads from central Asia, settle down as rulers of an empire in northern Iran.

↑ This carved staircase shows visitors to the Persian emperor in Persepolis.

Timeline of Alexander the Great

359 B.C. Philip II comes to power in Macedon.

343 Philip employs Aristotle as tutor to his son Alexander.

336 Alexander succeeds to the Macedonian throne.

334 Alexander invades Anatolia and defeats a Persian army.

333 Alexander defeats the Persians at the Issus River.

332 Alexander conquers Egypt.

331 After victory in the Battle of Gaugamela, Alexander takes control of the Persian Empire.

330 Alexander burns the palace of Persepolis.

Alexander was only 20 years old when he came to the throne of Macedon in 336 B.C., after the murder of his father Philip II. Philip had made his kingdom the most powerful state in Greece. He was about to invade the Persian Empire when he was killed.

Invasion of Persia

Alexander soon put his father's plan into action. In 334 B.C., he invaded and conquered Anatolia (present-day Turkey), which was a Persian province.

← Alexander conquered the Persian Empire with an army of only 30,000 men.

c.240 The Greek scholar Eratosthenes works out the circumference of Earth.

218 The Second Punic War begins; the Carthaginian general Hannibal crosses the Alps to invade Italy from the north.

230   220   210

219 Seleucid forces try to invade Palestine but are defeated by its Egyptian rulers.

216 Hannibal defeats the Romans at the Battle of Cannae.

Timeline (continued)

328 Alexander completes his conquest of Persia.

326 At the Indus River, an army revolt forces Alexander to give up plans to conquer India.

323 Alexander dies suddenly in Babylon.

322 Ptolemy, one of Alexander's generals, seizes Egypt.

320–301 Alexander's generals fight one another in the Wars of the Diadochi ("Wars of the Successors").

305 Ptolemy proclaims himself pharaoh of Egypt.

301 Seleucus establishes his hold over the eastern part of Alexander's empire, extending the Seleucid Kingdom, which will survive until 63 B.C.

He met and defeated two Persian armies, one of them led by King Darius III in person, before turning to Egypt—another Persian possession—which he conquered in 332 B.C.

Alexander headed into the heart of Darius's empire. He defeated his rival again before burning down Persepolis, the Persian capital. Darius was soon

Alexander conquered Persia and extended his empire as far as the Indus River. ↓

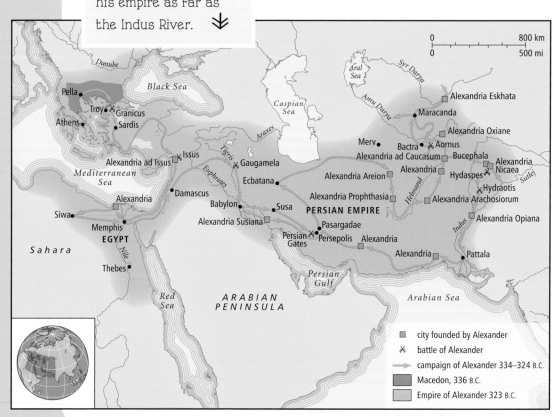

city founded by Alexander
✗ battle of Alexander
→ campaign of Alexander 334–324 B.C.
Macedon, 336 B.C.
Empire of Alexander 323 B.C.

TIMELINE
210–150 B.C.

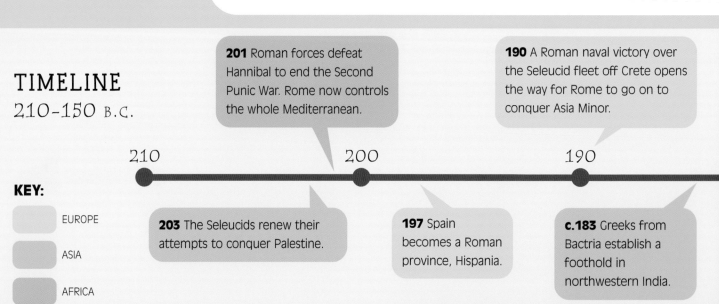

201 Roman forces defeat Hannibal to end the Second Punic War. Rome now controls the whole Mediterranean.

190 A Roman naval victory over the Seleucid fleet off Crete opens the way for Rome to go on to conquer Asia Minor.

210

200

190

KEY:

EUROPE

ASIA

AFRICA

203 The Seleucids renew their attempts to conquer Palestine.

197 Spain becomes a Roman province, Hispania.

c.183 Greeks from Bactria establish a foothold in northwestern India.

← The Indus River in Pakistan was as far as Alexander's men were prepared to go.

murdered by a Persian governor, angry about the king's military failures. For three years, the Macedonian army fought through central Asia. Alexander wanted to invade northern India, but his army had had enough. Alexander was forced to agree to return home.

Alexander died suddenly in 323 B.C. while planning his next campaign. His empire collapsed into chaos. His heirs were murdered, and his Macedonian generals fought to carve out kingdoms for themselves.

The Hellenistic Age

Alexander founded Greek cities in the lands he conquered, all the way from Alexandria in Egypt to Bactria (in present-day Afghanistan). As a result, the Greek language, together with Greek architecture, sculpture, and learning, dominated the ancient world for several centuries. Historians call this period the Hellenistic Age (from "Hellene," the word the Greeks used to describe themselves).

A Greek City in Egypt

Alexander founded a city at the mouth of the Nile and named it after himself. Alexandria became the leading city in the Greek world. It was home to the mathematician Euclid and the engineer Hero. Best known of the city's monuments was the lighthouse of Pharos, one of the Wonders of the Ancient World.

← Queen Cleopatra was the last of Egypt's Hellenistic rulers.

167 Followers of Judas Maccabeus revolt in Judah against attempts to outlaw Judaism.

164 The Maccabeans succeed in reestablishing Judaism in Judah.

170

160

150

171 Mithridates becomes king of the Parthians and begins building an empire.

c.150 Roman engineers invent concrete for building.

The Rise of Rome

Over 250 years, Rome rose to dominate first Italy and then the whole Mediterranean. But as Rome's territories grew, unrest at home led to dictatorship and civil war.

The ruins of the Forum in Rome. Similar structures can be found all over the former Roman Empire. →

TIMELINE
150–90 B.C.

146 Rome finally destroys Carthage; it is now master of the whole Mediterranean.

133 The tribune Tiberius Gracchus is killed, as part of the tension between plebeians and aristocrats.

150   140   130

KEY:

- EUROPE
- ASIA
- AFRICA

149 B.C. The Third Punic War begins.

133 The Roman Empire absorbs Pergamon, in modern Turkey.

125 Hipparchos, the first man to use longitude and latitude, dies.

⇐ Roman power expanded from Rome itself to Italy and the Mediterranean region, then north.

Timeline of Rome's Rise

494 B.C. Roman plebeians (commoners) appoint tribunes to protect their interests.

312 The first major Roman road, the Appian Way, is begun from Rome to Capua.

275 Victory over the Greek kingdom of Epiros confirms Rome's mastery of Italy.

241 Victory in the First Punic War (264 B.C.–241 B.C.) gives Rome control of Sicily.

218 Hannibal of Carthage starts the Second Punic War (218 B.C.–201 B.C.) by invading Italy across the Alps.

The ancestors of the Romans were immigrants from north of the Alps who spoke the language that was later to develop into Latin. They moved into central Italy in about 1000 B.C. and built villages on the Tiber River. By the eighth century B.C., the settlements had merged into the town of Rome.

Early Rome was ruled by kings, but it became a republic in 509 B.C. The republic was governed by two elected officials, called consuls, and by the Senate, a

102 The Romans put down revolts by the Germanic Cimbri and Teutones tribes.

110   100   90

c.100 Alexandria, in Egypt, becomes a center for Greek-style mosaics that are popular among wealthy Romans.

Timeline (continued)

203 Having failed to take Rome, Hannibal is recalled to Africa.

146 The Third Punic War (149 B.C.– 146 B.C.) ends with the destruction of Carthage.

71 A slave revolt led by a Thracian gladiator named Spartacus is crushed.

59 The general Pompey the Great forms an alliance with Marcus Crassus and Julius Caesar to win political power.

58–50 Caesar conquers Gaul and raids Britain and the German lands.

Augustus, the adopted → son and heir of Julius Caear, became the first emperor of Rome in 27 B.C.

body of aristocrats known as patricians. The commoners, or plebeians, later set up an assembly and elected officials called tribunes to protect their interests.

Conflict with Carthage

The new republic imposed its power over other Italian states by force and diplomacy. Conquered rivals were offered alliances, or even citizenship; in return, they had to pay taxes and provide soldiers for the Roman army. The Romans also consolidated their hold on Italy by founding colonies linked by a network of roads.

Alliances with Greek cities in southern Italy brought Rome into conflict with Carthage, on the North African coast. In the three Punic Wars (from the Latin *Punicus*, or "Phoenician," the nationality of Carthage's founders), Rome achieved naval supremacy, survived an invasion led by the general Hannibal, and (in 146 B.C.) destroyed Carthage itself.

End of the Republic

The defeat of Carthage opened the way for more conquests. Greece, Asia Minor, Syria, Palestine, and Gaul (modern-day France) all fell to Rome. At home, though,

TIMELINE
90–30 B.C.

c.80 The Greeks invent a calculator with gears for working out the calendar.

63 Pompey conquers Judea and incorporates it into Syria.

90   80   70

85 After revolting against Roman rule, Athens loses its political privileges.

64 The Roman general Pompey conquers Syria.

KEY:

EUROPE

ASIA

AFRICA

↑ Julius Caesar was assassinated by politicians opposed to his dictatorship.

the republican system was breaking down. The patricians created country estates worked by slaves. Landless peasants flocked to the cities or joined the army, where they provided the power base for military dictators: Lucius Sulla, Pompey the Great, and Julius Caesar.

After Caesar was murdered by plotters in 44 B.C., civil war broke out between his adopted son, Octavian, and Mark Antony, who planned to create a separate empire with Cleopatra, queen of Egypt. The defeat of Mark Antony's navy at Actium left Octavian as sole ruler of the Roman world. His new title "Augustus," meaning "revered one," would be used by Roman emperors for the next five centuries.

Timeline (continued)

49 Julius Caesar fights a civil war with the armies of Pompey.

45 On the death of Pompey, Caesar becomes sole ruler.

44 Caesar is assassinated by Romans unwilling to accept one-man rule.

43 Caesar's heir Octavian joins forces with Mark Antony and Marcus Lepidus to reconstitute the government.

37 Mark Antony flaunts his relationship with Cleopatra, queen of Egypt.

31 The defeat of Antony and Cleopatra at the naval Battle of Actium leaves Octavian master of the Roman world.

30 Antony and Cleopatra commit suicide.

27 Octavian assumes the name Augustus and takes authority over all Rome's territories.

58 Julius Caesar begins a 10-year campaign to conquer Gaul.

44 Julius Caesar is assassinated on his way to the Senate.

30 Rome takes Egypt after Antony and Cleopatra commit suicide.

50

40

30

53 The Parthians defeat Rome to take control of the Silk Road, the trade route linking the West to East Asia.

40 The Roman Senate crowns Herod the Great king of Judea.

31 Octavian defeats Antony and Cleopatra in the civil war after Caesar's death.

The Roman Empire

By the start of the second century A.D., Rome's empire stretched from England to Egypt and from Spain to Syria; never had so many peoples lived under one government.

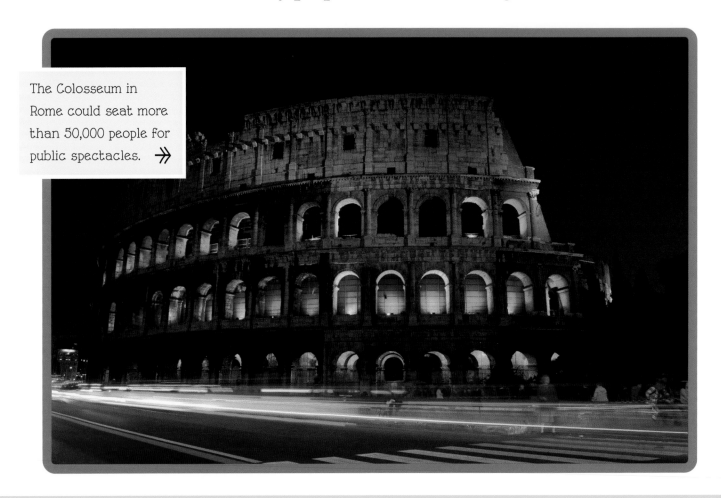

The Colosseum in Rome could seat more than 50,000 people for public spectacles. →

TIMELINE
30 B.C.–A.D. 30

27 Octavian takes the title Augustus, marking the start of Rome's imperial period.

c.10 Herod the Great uses concrete blocks to build the first harbor in the open sea, at Caesarea, in modern Israel.

4 Jesus Christ is probably born in Bethlehem, Judea.

30   20   10

KEY:

EUROPE

ASIA

AFRICA

30 B.C. Mark Antony and Cleopatra commit suicide.

c.0 Romans sailors use the regular monsoon winds to establish trade links with southern India.

The emperors kept Romans happy with spectacles like gladiatorial combats. ↓

When Augustus became Rome's first emperor, he claimed to restore republican government but kept all real power himself. He was supreme commander of the army, which included a new personal bodyguard, the Praetorian Guard. Augustus stamped out corruption, established a civil service, and rebuilt Rome. But his death exposed the weakness of a system that depended on the emperor's personal qualities for its success. Over the next 50 years, Rome's rulers included Caligula, who made his favorite horse a consul, and Nero, who murdered his mother and two of his wives.

The empire continued to grow, however. One reason was the efficiency of its administration. The empire's main prop, however, was the Roman army, which the most efficient fighting machine of its day; its legions, staffed

Timeline of the Roman Empire

27 B.C. Octavian takes the title of Augustus. The imperial period of Roman history is often dated from this year.

19 The Roman general Agrippa conquers Spain.

14 A.D. Augustus dies; Tiberius becomes emperor.

37 Tiberius is succeeded by the crazed Caligula.

41 Caligula is murdered by his own bodyguard, who replaces him with his uncle, Claudius.

43 Claudius conquers Britain.

54 Claudius dies and is replaced by Nero.

64 Fire destroys much of Rome.

← Trajan's column in Rome celebrated the military victories that increased the empire.

c.0 The Greek geographer Strabo makes a description of the known world.

14 Tiberius becomes emperor on the death of Augustus.

10

20

30

A.D. 9 German warriors wipe out three Roman legions; the Rhine River becomes the northern frontier of the empire.

c.30 Jesus Christ is crucified in Jerusalem.

Timeline (continued)

68 Nero is deposed by an army revolt.

80 The Colosseum is completed in Rome.

117 The empire reaches its largest extent under Trajan.

122 In Britain, work begins on Hadrian's Wall.

138 Antoninus begins a long reign of peace and prosperity.

161 Marcus Aurelius succeeds Antoninus.

212 All free adult males in the empire are granted Roman citizenship.

At its height, the empire covered more than 3 million square miles (5 million sq km). ➤➤

by career soldiers, rarely failed to defeat their less-organized opponents. Britain was conquered in A.D. 43, Dacia (Romania) in 106, Armenia and Parthia (northwest Persia) by 117. Taxes and tributes poured into Rome. The emperors spent some of this wealth on massive building projects. They also used their wealth to buy public support, handing out free grain and paying for gladiatorial games.

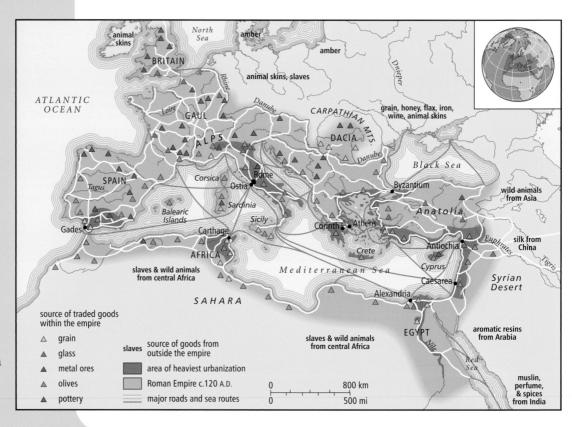

TIMELINE
A.D. 30–90

KEY:

EUROPE

ASIA

AFRICA

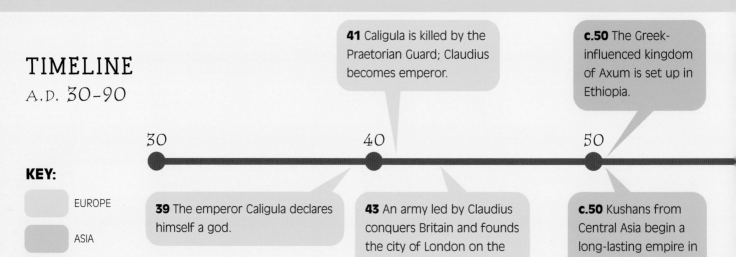

41 Caligula is killed by the Praetorian Guard; Claudius becomes emperor.

c.50 The Greek-influenced kingdom of Axum is set up in Ethiopia.

30   40   50

39 The emperor Caligula declares himself a god.

43 An army led by Claudius conquers Britain and founds the city of London on the Thames River.

c.50 Kushans from Central Asia begin a long-lasting empire in northwestern India.

⇐ Pompeii in Italy was buried by a volcanic eruption in A.D. 79. The ash helped preserve the city.

Roman Roads

"They have built paved roads throughout the country," the Greek Strabo noted in the first century A.D. Road building was one of the Romans' great achievements. The highways helped their legions march over 30 miles (50 km) a day. The stone roads rested on beds of sand and gravel; the surface was sloped so rainwater ran off into gutters.

⇐ Roads were built by gangs of soldiers directed by engineers.

Life in Rome's Provinces

If Rome grew rich from its conquests, many of its provinces also prospered. In return for paying taxes, their citizens received the protection of the world's strongest military power. In regions where city living had long been established, merchants found a new export market for their goods. In more remote areas, the Romans introduced the benefits of urban living. Most large provincial towns had Roman-style public buildings, including amphitheaters, law courts, and public baths.

c.60 Emperor Nero bans the import of pepper to try to stop Romans spending so much money on imports from India.

79 An eruption of Vesuvius in Italy buries the Roman towns of Pompeii and Herculaneum.

70

80

90

61 The British queen Boudicca (Boadicea) leads the Iceni tribe in a revolt against Roman rule.

c.80 The Romans boost agriculture in North Africa to produce more wheat, olives, and grapes.

c.90 Artists in Gandhara, in modern Pakistan, create Greek-influenced work, including statues of Buddha.

Roman Engineering

The Romans relied on their army to increase their territory, but engineers were vital to keeping the sprawling empire together.

The Pont du Gard carried water across the Gard River in France. ⇒

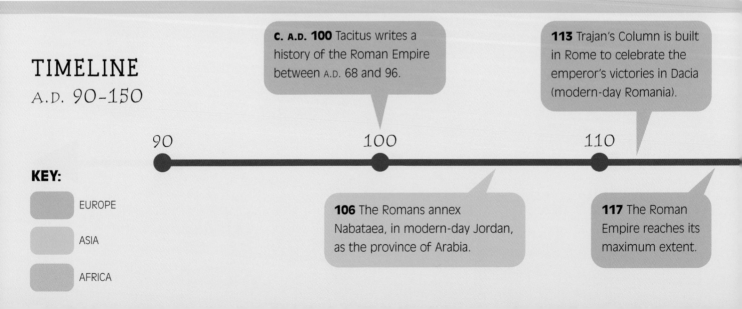

TIMELINE
A.D. 90–150

KEY:
- EUROPE
- ASIA
- AFRICA

c. A.D. 100 Tacitus writes a history of the Roman Empire between A.D. 68 and 96.

113 Trajan's Column is built in Rome to celebrate the emperor's victories in Dacia (modern-day Romania).

90

100

110

106 The Romans annex Nabataea, in modern-day Jordan, as the province of Arabia.

117 The Roman Empire reaches its maximum extent.

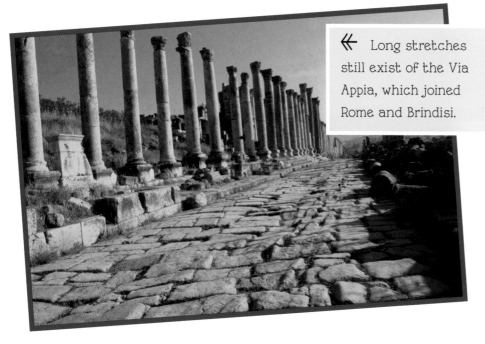

← Long stretches still exist of the Via Appia, which joined Rome and Brindisi.

Timeline of Roman Engineering

312 B.C. Via Appia begun.

c.150 Roman engineers work out how to make and use concrete.

c.20 The Pont du Gard is built near Nîmes, France.

A.D. 27 Work begins on the Pantheon in Rome; it is completed just over 100 years later.

c.50 The aqueduct is built at Segovia, Spain.

52 The Aqua Claudia is completed in Rome.

128 Roman builders complete Hadrian's Wall across the northern border of England.

At their peak, Roman highways stretched over 50,000 miles (80,000 km)—enough to reach twice around the world. Great military roads spread out from Rome. A system ran along the Mediterranean coast in North Africa; in Gaul (France), roads radiated from Lyon; and in Britain, London was the hub of the system.

The first Roman road was the Via Appia (Appian Way), built in 312 B.C. and later extended to the coast at Brundisium (present-day Brindisi). Other roads soon followed, such as the Via Flaminia from Rome to the Adriatic coast.

← Great stone aqueducts carried water from the hills into Rome. The city's first aqueduct was build in 312 B.C.

134 Roman troops in eastern Turkey repel an attack by peoples from southern Russia.

c.140 Death of Juvenal, a poet who wrote satirical works about Rome's problems.

130

140

150

128 Hadrian's Wall is completed against northern England.

c.150 In western India a carver creates the earliest known inscription in Sanskrit.

The Arch

Roman engineers developed the use of the arch. The arch was the strongest means of supporting a wall or a roof. The arch was built over a wooden scaffold that held it up. After the arch was completed with a central wedge-shaped keystone, the structure held itself up. The scaffold was taken down.

The arch was the basis of techniques such as the vault. ↓

Public baths and drinking fountains were features of many towns. ⇒

Pioneering Road Builders

The Romans built roads mainly for couriers, traders, and officials. They were also useful for moving troops rapidly in case of trouble with local people. Wherever possible, the roads followed a straight line. For a major highway, the engineers first dug parallel drainage ditches, then excavated a shallow trench between them, which they filled with layers of sand, mortar, and stone to form the foundation. They topped the road with a surface pavement of stone slabs or cobbles set in mortar.

TIMELINE
A.D. 150–210

161 Marcus Aurelius, known as a philosopher, becomes emperor.

173 Egyptian shepherds rebel against Roman rule but are crushed.

150   160   170

168 Death of Claudius Ptolemy, the Egyptian astronomer who popularized the Earth-centered view of the universe, the Ptolemaic System.

KEY:

EUROPE

ASIA

AFRICA

On marshy ground, the whole road was raised above the countryside. Some major roads in Italy had stone curbs 8 inches (20 cm) high on each side, with side lanes outside them that operated as one-way streets. Drivers of fast chariots could achieve 75 miles (120 km) a day; freight wagons covered 15 miles (25 km) a day.

As the Roman Empire crumbled, so did its roads, owing to a lack of maintenance. Later road builders sometimes took over the Roman routes, as can still be seen by straight stretches on any road map of England.

Building Aqueducts

As Roman towns and cities increased in size, demand grew for water for drinking or bathing and to wash in. To bring in the water, Roman engineers built aqueducts. An aqueduct may be an open or closed culvert, a tunnel through a hill, or—at its most spectacular—a bridge across a valley.

Between 312 B.C. and A.D. 200, engineers built 11 aqueducts to take water into Rome, some from more than 56 miles (90 km) away. The water flowed along by gravity. Other Roman aqueducts in Italy, France, Greece, and Spain are still used today.

The Pantheon

The Pantheon is a temple that still stands in Rome. When it was completed around A.D. 128, its 142-foot (43-m) dome was the largest in the world. Engineers used concrete to keep the roof as light as possible. The dome gets thinner in the middle for the same reason. At the top, the concrete is only about a foot thick.

← The Pantheon in Rome was completed between A.D. 118 and 128.

193 Septimius Severus comes to the throne and puts down a challenge from the governor of Syria.

c.200 A collection of Jewish oral law, the Mishnah, takes its final form.

190

200

210

c.190 An artist in Rome carves one of the earliest known examples of Christian art.

197 Roman troops in Britain declare Clodius Albinus emperor, but he is defeated by emperor Septimius Severus.

c.203 Septimius Severus orders a persecution of Christians in the empire.

The Spread of Christianity

Jesus Christ preached in Palestine, then part of the Roman Empire, in the early first century A.D. before he was executed for his political and religious views.

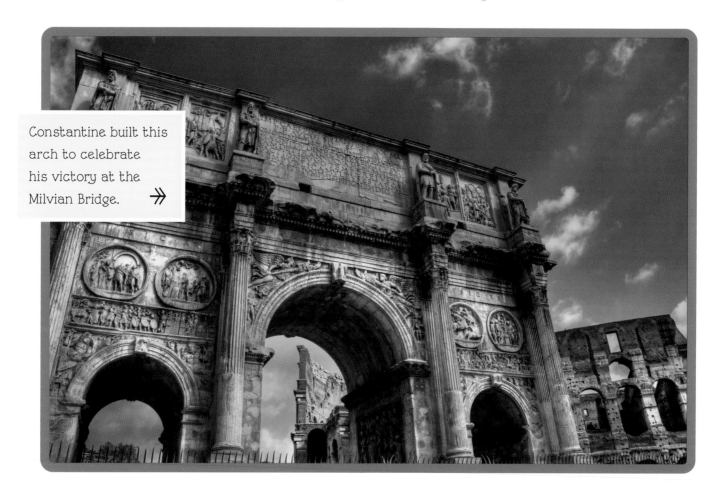

Constantine built this arch to celebrate his victory at the Milvian Bridge. ⇒

TIMELINE
A.D. 210–270

219 Babylonia becomes the center of Jewish cultural life.

224 The Persian Ardashir I overthrows the Parthians to found the Sassanian Empire.

210

220

230

KEY:

EUROPE

ASIA

AFRICA

A.D. 212 Roman citizenship is extended to everyone living in the empire—mainly in an attempt to raise more taxes.

c.224 Kushan territory in Bactria and northern India is seized by Sassanians

240 Shapur I becomes emperor of the Sassanians.

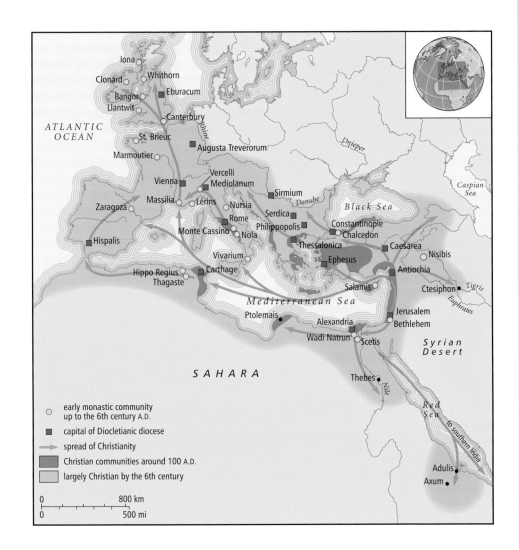

← Christianity spread
from its origins in the
eastern Mediterranean
across the Roman Empire.

Timeline of Early Christianity

c.30 A.D. Jesus is crucified in Jerusalem.

c.46–62 Paul makes four missionary journeys, founding churches and visiting Rome.

c.60–100 The four Gospels, telling the story of Jesus's life and death, are written down.

64 Nero executes Christians after a great fire in Rome.

c.67 Paul is executed in Rome.

252 A council of bishops reaffirms the pope's position at the head of the church.

303 Diocletian unleashes a violent persecution of Christians.

Jesus's followers, the Christians, believed that he was the Messiah, or son of God, who had risen from the dead. They began meeting in small groups to spread the news of his resurrection. In the first decades after his

250 An imperial edict against them forces many Christians into hiding.

267 The Germanic Goths from the Black Sea raid into the Roman Empire in Thrace, Macedonia, and Greece.

250

260

270

248 In Alexandria in Egypt, citizens riot against Christians.

260 The Roman emperor Valerian is defeated by the Persians at Edessa in eastern Turkey.

269 The Palmyran queen Zenobia conquers Egypt and other Roman territory in Asia Minor.

c.305 St. Anthony founds colonies of hermits in the Egyptian desert.

312 Constantine adopts the symbol of the cross at the Battle of the Milvian Bridge.

325 Constantine presides over the first General Council of the Church, held at Nicaea.

405 St. Jerome completes the first Latin translation of the Bible.

c.430–460 St. Patrick preaches Christianity in Ireland.

c.480 St. Benedict is born in Italy. The Benedictine rule he will devise for his monastery at Monte Cassino, dividing the monk's day into set periods for work and prayer, will become the model for monastic life in western Europe.

Constantine the Great was the first Roman emperor to become Christian. →

In this carving, the cross is combined with a symbol that combines the Greek initials of Christ's name. →

death, the new religion spread outside Palestine. Its first great missionary was Paul of Tarsus, a Roman citizen from a wealthy Jewish family. Paul traveled throughout the eastern Mediterranean as far as Rome itself to preach the Christian gospel to Jews and non-Jews alike.

Christians and Rome

The Roman authorities did not trust the early Christians because they refused to follow the official state religion. In A.D. 64, the Emperor Nero blamed them for starting a fire that destroyed much of the city of Rome. Many Christians were rounded up and executed. It was the first of a series of mass

TIMELINE
A.D. 270–330

272 Queen Zenobia is captured by the Romans; she spends the rest of her life in Rome.

286 Facing barbarian attacks, Diocletian splits the Roman empire into western and eastern parts with separate emperors.

270   280   290

KEY:

EUROPE

ASIA

AFRICA

c.270 Saint Anthony moves into the Egyptian desert; he is one of the first and most influential Christian hermits.

287 A Roman naval commander, Marcus Aurelius Carausius, rebels against the rule of Diocletian, but he is defeated after nine years.

persecutions of Christians over the next 250 years. As a result, the early Christians lived and worshiped in secret, adopting signs such as the sign of a fish to identify their places of worship to each other. These signs can still be seen carved on the walls of the catacombs, or underground cemeteries, in Rome.

The last great persecution of Christians took place under Emperor Diocletian in 303. Soon afterward the Emperor Constantine adopted a policy of toleration throughout the empire. From then on, Christianity could be practiced openly, and the faith grew rapidly.

Constantine the Great

In 312, Constantine defeated his fellow emperor, Maxentius, in battle after seeing a vision of the cross. In 313, he legalized Christianity in the Western Empire. He supported Christians throughout the empire and ordered many churches to be built, including St. Peter's at Rome. Constantine was baptized on his deathbed in 337.

← Saint Peter's in Rome was said to be built on the grave of the saint.

306 Constantine becomes joint Roman emperor in the west.

313 In the Edict of Milan, Constantine grants toleration to Christians in the western empire.

324 Constantine becomes the sole emperor.

310

320

330

303 Diocletian begins the last persecution of the Christians.

320 In India, Chandragupta I creates a Hindu kingdom on the Ganges Plain, creating the Gupta dynasty.

330 Constantine founds the city of Constantinople on the strait between Europe and Asia.

The Fall of Rome

In A.D. 476, a German general named Odoacer overthrew the last Roman emperor in the west, ending nearly 500 years of imperial rule.

This Roman coin shows a barbarian warrior holding a severed head. →

TIMELINE
A.D. 330–390

348 The Sassanians defeat the Romans at Singara but fail to drive them from Mesopotamia.

c.350 King Ezana of Axum becomes the first known Christian in sub-Saharan Africa.

330   340   350

KEY:

EUROPE

A.D. 335 In India, the Gupta king Samudragupta begins a series of major military campaigns.

c.350 White Huns begin raiding into Persia from the east.

ASIA

AFRICA

← Roman troops prepare for battle in these carvings from the Arch of Constantine.

An Unstable Period

For centuries, the Romans traded with the Germanic tribes settled beyond the empire's northern frontier. In the third century, however, relations worsened. German raiders, attracted by the empire's wealth, made frequent raids across its borders. On the eastern frontier, the Romans were under threat from the Sassanian rulers of Persia.

An Unstable Period

After 150 years of stability, the Romans found themselves almost constantly at war. Emperors relied on the support of the army, which was often withdrawn. In all, 66 emperors ruled between 235 and 284, reigning on average for less than two years

Timeline of the Fall of Rome

A.D. 235 A chaotic period begins in which the army declare 43 different emperors in 35 years.

240 The empire is attacked on several fronts: in Africa, in Europe, and in Persia.

256 The Franks cross the Rhine frontier into the empire.

284 Diocletian comes to power and begins to restore the authority of the emperors.

286 Diocletian splits the empire into two.

293 Diocletian establishes two rulers in each half of the empire.

← Diocletian, shown here with his three imperial coregents, was a fierce persecutor of early Christians.

c.372 The nomadic Huns from Central Asia conquer the Ostrogoths in the Black Sea region.

370   380   390

361 The Emperor Julian tries to revive paganism in the Roman Empire.

380 Chandragupta II takes over the Gupta Empire, which he will bring to its peak.

Timeline (continued)

324 Constantine reunites the empire.

378 Visigoths kill the Emperor Valens at the Battle of Adrianople.

406 A barbarian army crosses the Rhine and invades deep into Gaul.

441–451 Huns invade the empire.

455 A Vandal army sacks Rome.

476 Odoacer declares himself king of Italy and is recognized by the Eastern Emperor Zeno.

480 Julius Nepos, the last western emperor, dies.

488 Zeno urges the Ostrogoth Theodoric to invade Italy.

493 Odoacer is murdered; Italy becomes part of the Kingdom of the Ostrogoths.

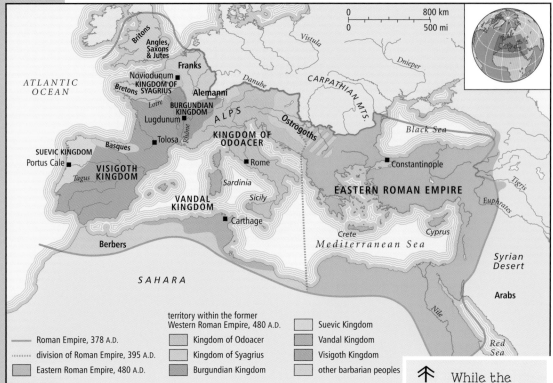

each; all but one died violently. The cost of raising armies and defending the frontiers brought financial ruin.

In 284, Diocletian became emperor. He decided that the empire was too large to be ruled by one man and divided it into eastern and western halves; each half had two *augusti*, or co-emperors. He also doubled the size of the army. As a result, taxes rose, forcing farmers to leave the land.

While the western lands fell apart, the eastern empire remained largely intact.

TIMELINE
A.D. 390–450

395 Theodosius dies; the empire is permanently divided into eastern and western parts.

407 The Roman garrison quits Britain, which leaves the empire.

410 A Visigoth army led by Alaric sacks Rome.

390   400   410

391 The Emperor Theodosius I officially ends paganism within the Roman Empire.

402 Ravenna, on Italy's east coast, replaces Rome as capital of the western empire.

413 Emperor Theodosius II fortifies Constantinople with strong city walls.

KEY:

EUROPE

ASIA

AFRICA

Famines were frequent, and starvation caused the population to fall, especially in the western half of the empire. The shortage of manpower led the Romans to start recruiting German mercenaries (soldiers fighting for pay) into their armies.

The End of the Empire

In the late fourth century, the Huns burst out of Central Asia into the lands west of the Black Sea, setting up a kingdom in Hungary. Their raids caused panic among the German tribes, who fled across the Roman frontier. Over the next century, the Germans carved out kingdoms in Gaul, Spain, North Africa, and Italy. The eastern half of the Roman Empire clung on for another millennium as the Byzantine Empire, but by A.D. 500, all traces of Rome's once-great authority had vanished from western Europe.

← Vandals crossed from North Africa to sack Rome in A.D. 455.

The Huns

The Huns earned a fearsome reputation. Their war leader Attila was known as "the scourge of God." He led the Huns through the Balkans to threaten Constantinople. In 451, the Huns invaded Gaul, but a combined army of Romans and Visigoths defeated them at the Battle of Châlons. Attila led another invasion of Italy but died in 453. Without him, his empire quickly collapsed.

↑ Attila the Hun remains a byword for extreme savagery.

431 Vandals from Spain capture the Roman town of Hippo in North Africa.

c.450 Anglo-Saxons, originally from northern Germany and Denmark, begin to settle in England.

430   440   450

439 The Vandals capture the city of Carthage and make it their capital.

Glossary

Acropolis The rocky hill that overlooks the city of Athens and on which the Parthenon was built.

amphitheater An open-air venue, similar to a modern sports stadium, where gladiatorial contests, parades, and chariot races were held.

aristocrat A nobleman who ruled the city-states of Greece and Rome.

citizenship In ancient Greece and Rome, citizenship granted a person many advantages, such as the right to vote or run for public office. Anyone whose parents were citizens was automatically granted citizenship, but others had to earn citizenship by serving in the army. Women and freed slaves typically could not become full citizens.

city-state An independent country that consists of a self-governing city and the surrounding countryside.

dark age A period in which there is little technological or cultural activity of lasting significance.

democracy Literally "power by the people," a system of government whereby policies were determined by popular vote.

dictator A ruler who holds absolute power, but who governs without the consent of the majority of the people.

golden age A period of prosperity, cultural activity, and technological progress.

hellenistic Influenced by Greek culture or politics. Hellenistic civilizations included many of the kingdoms around the Mediterranean Sea, as well as Alexander the Great's former empire.

Parthenon Temple dedicated to the goddess Athena that was built in the 5th century B.C. atop the Acropolis.

peninsula A narrow strip of land that projects into a body of water.

Persia Foreign rival to the Greek city-states. Until the 5th century B.C., it was the world's largest empire.

philosophy The study of subjects such as ethics, human relationships, and the nature of thought and reality

Further Reading

Books

Baker, Simon. *Ancient Rome: The Rise and Fall of an Empire*. London: BBC Books, 2007.

Barker, Graeme, and Tim Rasmussen. *The Etruscans*. Oxford: Wiley-Blackwell, 2000.

Barnes, Jonathan. *Aristotle: A Very Short Introduction*. New York: Oxford University Press, 2001.

Bauer, Susan Wise. *The History of the Ancient World: From the Earliest Accounts to the Fall of Rome*. New York: W. W. Norton, 2007.

Clark, Gillian. *Christianity and Roman Society*. New York: Cambridge University Press, 2004.

Filde, Alan, and Joan Fletcher. *Alexander the Great: Son of the Gods*. Los Angeles: Getty Publications, 2004.

Gibbon, Edward. *The History of the Decline and Fall of the Roman Empire*. New York: Penguin Classics, 2001.

Landeis, J. G. *Engineering in the Ancient World*. Berkeley: University of California Press, 2000.

Martin, Thomas R., *Ancient Greece: From Prehistoric to Hellenistic Times*. New Haven: Yale University Press, 2000.

Rodgers, Nigel. *The Illustrated Encyclopedia of the Roman Empire*. London: Lorenz Books, 2008.

Traina, Giusto. *428 AD: An Ordinary Year at the End of the Roman Empire*. Princeton, NJ: Princeton University Press, 2009.

Warry, John Gibson. *Warfare in the Classical World*. London: Barnes & Noble, 2000.

Web Sites

www.ancientgreece.com/s/Main_Page/
Offers information about Greek history, culture, mythology, and geography

http://ancienthistory.about.com/od/ basics101/tp/061308famouspeople.htm
Information about the most important people in classical history

www.bbc.co.uk/history/ancient/greeks/
BBC online guide to the history of Ancient Greece and Hellenistic civilization

www.bbc.co.uk/history/ancient/ romans/
BBC online guide to the history of the Roman Empire

Index